Shaping our lives – from outset to outcome

What people think of the social care services they use

Shaping Our Lives National User Network, Black User Group (West London), Ethnic Disabled Group Emerged (Manchester), Footprints and Waltham Forest Black Mental Health Service User Group (North London), and Service Users' Action Forum (Wakefield)

JR
JOSEPH
ROWNTREE
FOUNDATION

The **Joseph Rowntree Foundation** has supported this project as part of its programme of research and innovative development projects, which it hopes will be of value to policy makers, practitioners and service users. The facts presented and views expressed in this report are, however, those of the authors and not necessarily those of the Foundation.

Joseph Rowntree Foundation
The Homestead, 40 Water End, York YO30 6WP
Website: www. jrf.org.uk

Shaping
Our Lives

Michael Turner
Shaping Our Lives project worker 1996–2002

Shaping Our Lives is a national research and development project run by service users. It is working to establish a national network of organisations controlled by service users including: disabled people, older people, people with learning difficulties and users and survivors of mental health services. Shaping Our Lives are also working to make links with a wide range of other service users.

A CIP catalogue record for this report is available from the British Library.

ISBN 1 85935 113 1   (paperback)
ISBN 1 85935 114 X   (pdf: available at www.jrf.org.uk)

Cover design by Adkins Design

Prepared and printed by:
York Publishing Services Ltd
64 Hallfield Road
Layerthorpe
York YO31 7ZQ
Tel: 01904 430033; Fax: 01904 430868; Website: www.yps-publishing.co.uk

Further copies of this report, or any other JRF publication, can be obtained either from the JRF website (www.jrf.org.uk/bookshop/) or from our distributor, York Publishing Services Ltd, at the above address.

Dedication

This report is dedicated to the memory of John McKevitt.

John had co-ordinated the work of the Service Users' Action Forum's input to this project and had made a huge contribution to the involvement of older people in Wakefield and at a national level.

He frequently made the point that, when working with older people, you cannot be sure how long they are going to be around for. His work on Shaping Our Lives and other projects showed how great a contribution older people can make while they are with us.

John will be remembered with much fondness and great respect by those of us who were fortunate enough to work with him.

The project would not have been possible without the enthusiastic participation of the members of the four development projects.

The co-ordinators of each of the four groups played an essential role in getting things started and, in sometimes difficult circumstances, ensuring that they continued through to the end of the project: Pauline Abott-Butler, Patricia Chambers, Pam John and John McKevitt.

Contents

Acknowledgements

Thanks are also due to the following:

- the Joseph Rowntree Foundation's (JRF's) advisory panel for the project for advice, guidance and, most importantly, energy and enthusiasm for the work we were doing: Sue Balloch, Don Brand, Claire Crawley, Simeela Khaliq, Claudia Mark, Reg McLaughlin, Hazel Qureshi and Alex O'Neil of JRF

- the Shaping Our Lives management team: Peter Beresford, Phil Brough, June Sadd and Peter Williams

- for administrative support: Fung-Yee Lee and Rose Freeman of the National Institute for Social Work

- for other guidance and support, and ensuring that the project had a base: Daphne Statham, director of the National Institute for Social Workers (NISW).

PART I
PROJECT OVERVIEW AND CONCLUSIONS

1 Introduction

The idea for Shaping Our Lives (SOL) to run development projects came out of the desire to test the ideas and findings of the first phase of the project in practice in 'real-life' situations.

Shaping Our Lives' first phase was a relatively small-scale research project carried out from 1996–98. It involved a series of focus group meetings with different types of groups of service users, which examined their views on the concept of outcomes and their perspectives on the outcomes in their lives. The project was based on the principle of working across different types of service users, i.e. disabled people, older people, people with learning difficulties and users/survivors of mental health services.

Following these focus meetings, a group of service users was established (which was named the Shaping Our Lives National User Group) which had the opportunity to give these issues more detailed consideration over an extended period of time.

The key findings that came out of this phase of the project were as follows.

- *Value of outcomes*: users recognised the value of evaluating services in terms of their outcomes, but they saw it as essential that users' views were primary in this process and that the evaluation included the subjective perspectives of individual users. They recognised that such work could be supported by an element of objective measures, for example, a mental health service user suggested that effective services could be measured in relation to spending on drugs and that effective support would lead to less spending on drugs.

- *Difficulty identifying outcomes*: some users had some initial difficulty with the idea of looking at services in terms of outcomes or results. This was certainly not because the issue of outcomes was beyond service users. It appeared to be the case that, where services were poor and not being provided at an adequate level, users found it very difficult to determine the outcome of the service.

- *Outcomes for users of direct payments*: in contrast with the previous point, people in receipt of direct payments had very clear ideas about the outcomes that they had from the support that they arranged. This clearly showed the effectiveness and importance of direct payments – and pointed to the challenge for traditional services to provide a similar level of choice and empowerment by delivering the outcomes sought by service users.

- *Negative outcomes*: we found some clear examples of negative outcomes, which were characterised by being associated with services that did not meet the wishes of the user and usually disempowered, or added to the disempowerment, of the user.

- *Outcomes and process*: the process of getting a service and the way in which it is delivered can have a major impact on a user's experience of a service. These experiences include problems such as poor access to services, delays in service provision, poor treatment from service providers, lack of consultation or consultation which is ignored or not acted upon. Such experiences have an impact on the outcome of the service and are not detached from the outcome in users' perceptions. This view is contrary to the prevailing view among academics and professionals, who have focused primarily on outcomes in terms of the end result of a service.

- *A holistic approach*: many service users have needs that fall beyond the current limits of social care services. Some of these needs are those that may or may not be recorded as unmet in the current system, but there are other issues as well that are beyond this. Looking at outcomes from users' perspectives involves taking a holistic perspective and considering issues such as housing, transport, employment, income and benefits, and broader issues around discrimination and equality. The need to consider such issues illustrates how service users want to look at their lives and their needs as a whole, which is difficult with the current way that most social care services are organised.

The desire to test these ideas in practice resulted in this second phase of work carried out in conjunction with four local groups of service users:

- the Black User Group run by black mental health service users and survivors in the London Boroughs of Hammersmith and Fulham and Ealing

- Ethnic Disabled Group Emerged (EDGE)

- Footprints and Waltham Forest Black Mental Health Service User Group (North London)

- the Service Users' Action Forum, which is run by older people in Wakefield.

Each of the four groups has been a project in its own right and their reports are included with this report of the project as a whole. As well as feeding into this report, the local reports have been distributed locally to health and social services and other service providers in their areas to inform them about the work.

The role of this report is to bring together the overall findings of the project as a whole and to identify the common issues that have come out of what has probably been among the first projects of this type. The report also examines the process of the projects, looking at the lessons that can be learnt for other groups undertaking work in this field and some of the problems that have been encountered during the project.

The project should be seen as a start to work by service users in this area. It has been a good start but it has still been a relatively small project with limited resources. There is now the need to build on the experiences of this work and the lessons that have been learned, and to take them to other service users, service providers, planners and politicians.

Shaping Our Lives has now been given funding by the Department of Health to establish the Shaping Our Lives National User Network to support and promote user involvement at a national level. The Network will be promoting and building on the lessons from this project in many aspects of its work.

2 Setting up the local projects

The selection of groups to work with to establish the development projects took place during 1998–99 during an interim phase for Shaping Our Lives, which involved completing some work from the first project and thorough planning for the next stage.

A number of local groups were approached and initial discussions took place with seven groups to be a part of this project. They had responded to a mailing to the 300 organisations on the Shaping Our Lives database and to direct approaches from the project worker.

A specific mailing was also sent to black and ethnic community user groups on the database, which stressed our aim to include at least one black organisation in the project. This led to contact with the three black groups that took part in the project.

There was a commitment in the funding application to the Joseph Rowntree Foundation to include at least one group of older people in the project. Several approaches were made to older people's groups but there was interest only from the one that was to take part in the project.

These four groups were in a position to go forward when it became necessary to apply for funding for the main project to get under way.

The four projects

- Black User Group (BUG) (West London with participants from the London Boroughs of Hammersmith and Fulham and Ealing): this is a small, informal group of mental health service users that meets on a weekly basis for social activities and mutual support at a centre for black people. There have been around ten people participating in this group – six men and four women. The co-ordinator of the group was the point of contact for the project. In a reflection of this loose-knit structure, a core of five people in the group opted to share the writing of the reports of the meetings between them, although in practice the key-worker has had a leading role in this work.

- EDGE – Ethnic Disabled Group Emerged (Manchester): this is quite a large group of black disabled people, which itself provides services and support to people. It had originally planned to have up to 50 people working on the project in two groups, but the actual number involved was 24.

- Footprints (UK) and Waltham Forest Black Mental Health Service User Group (North London): Footprints is an independent voluntary organisation working with black mental health service users and run by a worker with experience as a user. It brought together this group of 20 people who regularly use a drop-in centre. Around a quarter of the group were male. Attendance at this group did fluctuate, but only slightly and at each meeting there were new people wanting to attend.

- Service Users' Action Forum (Wakefield): this is a network of older people associated with but independent of the local Age Concern group. Twelve people took part in this project – six men and six women. Membership remained constant; although one member and her husband became unable to attend meetings, they remained involved through visits by the worker.

The fact that priority had been given to black users and groups of older people when designing the project meant that there was not the mix of groups we originally anticipated. However, the fact that these groups constitute some of the least well represented people in the user movement made these four projects a valuable focus for initial work on outcomes with them. Starting with groups that have often been excluded from new work or brought into it only at a later stage has also meant that Shaping Our Lives has ensured that marginalised groups are part of this work from the outset.

It had been intended that Shaping Our Lives would be able to support the three other organisations that had also been discussing running projects to take the work forward. In the event, none of the groups found themselves able to pursue the work.

In looking at the start of the project, it should be noted that there was some delay following the initial approval of the grant and being able to go ahead with the project. After the grant was approved, and the four groups were informed that work could begin, it became necessary for SOL to negotiate the terms of the advisory panel for the project with the Joseph Rowntree Foundation. This delayed the project for several months initially, and then for a further period, as the groups had to re-engage the participants who had earlier identified their interest in the work.

3 Methodology

Getting started

In setting up the four groups, the aim was to give each group as much choice and control as possible over the project and how it was run. The groups were given a 'blank sheet' and asked to do work around user perspectives on outcomes in the way that they thought would be most appropriate.

This turned out to be too difficult for the groups to work with in practice. The idea of work on outcomes proved to be so new that the groups wanted a firmer idea of what was involved and what they should be doing. This meant that the project worker drew an initial plan for each group that was broadly similar, with the work structured around a series of five meetings over one year.

The first meeting was designated as a training session to introduce participants to the concept of outcomes and what the project was trying to achieve.

The second session was intended to enable people to apply the ideas from the first meeting to their own situations and the three follow-up meetings would look at changes that had taken place.

Once the projects started, they naturally began to diverge and new methods began to emerge, with two of the groups having key differences:

- *Service Users' Action Forum*: previous work indicated that older people found using a diary a good way to record important issues and changes, and this was adopted for this project. The group also agreed that it was important to meet more frequently than originally planned to give participants a proper sense of continuity. As a result, the group held its meetings over a period of nine months rather than the proposed 12.

- *EDGE*: the group here indicated that black users would prefer to discuss issues individually rather than in a group. This meant that the worker here has played a very active role in carrying out home visits and taking up issues on behalf of the individual service users. It also meant that the group's work was more individualised.

Principles for the meetings

One of the issues that was put to Shaping Our Lives during the first phase of research was that service users should be paid for taking part in research projects.

This was taken on board during the planning of the development projects and the budgets included payments for each service user who attended a meeting. This was in addition to expenses and the provision of lunch at the meetings. These arrangements are crucial to ensuring that service users who took part in the projects felt that their contribution was recognised and valued.

Each group also used a set of rules for their meetings. These involved respecting other participants' views and treating information given by individuals as confidential.

The high level of continued interest by members of each of the groups seems to indicate that these principles have been successful in encouraging and maintaining people's involvement in the work.

The first sessions: introducing users to outcomes

In the light of the initial project's finding that service users took some time to take on the idea of looking at services in terms of their outcomes, each of the groups began the project with a training session introducing people to the idea of outcomes and how they relate to their lives.

The training session was constructed around the Shaping Our Lives video which features a variety of service users describing their lives and the outcomes they are seeking to achieve. Other key parts of the training included exercises in looking at participants' typical days and what their ideal day would include. This seemed to work well and served as an effective way of getting participants to think about outcomes, their lives and their aspirations.

The typical day was not unusual ... None of the users felt that their day was a waste. (BUG)

Using the video had benefits and limitations. The variety of people featured in the video in terms of different types of service user and ethnic diversity helped participants to identify with the issues being discussed. However, the emphasis on people with physical impairments and issues such as direct payments made it difficult for some of the groups to relate fully to the video.

There is certainly a need for more focused video and printed material, and this project has generated a significant amount of new information that could form the basis for such material. This needs to be developed in collaboration with other agencies that have more expertise in training than is currently available within the project.

Work outside the meetings

Having started with a remit, to look at outcomes, all of the groups became active, to varying degrees, in working to influence the outcomes of the groups themselves, both for the individuals in the groups and the service users represented by the groups.

There was some variation in the way that they approached this action. The Action Forum took a strong, proactive line on all of the issues that were dealt with in the meetings. This was probably a development of an existing campaigning stance and hence the co-ordinator of the group actively lobbied the local health and social services, the local council and other service providers from early on in the project.

The Black User Group secured a meeting with representatives of the local health trust and social services department at the end of its series of

meetings. This gave the group's co-ordinator, with support from the SOL project worker, an opportunity to present the issues that had emerged from the meetings. The response was generally favourable, with agreement to examine issues that were within their control, but the point was made that issues such as high turnover of staff are beyond their control.

EDGE and the Footprints group took a slightly different and more individualised approach on many issues. The worker at EDGE took something of a 'caseworker' approach, which probably grew out of the more individualised emphasis of this project as a whole. Hence there was work on individual users' benefits and housing problems. Some of the issues did affect a number of people whom the project worked with, though these issues came out of the themed meetings held in addition to the visits to users' homes. In particular, this led to work on domiciliary care and raised awareness of EDGE's own service in this area. On transport issues, it led to increased awareness of the Dial-a-Ride service for disabled people.

Footprints particularly picked up on members' desire to develop their skills in regard to employment. Contact was made for interested members with the Disability Employment Adviser at the local Job Centre for information and assistance with training and employment issues. Members of the group also identified an interest in having access to computers to develop their skills, and the co-ordinator and SOL project worker successfully obtained funding from the Community Fund's small grants scheme to provide £5,000 of equipment.

It is important to note that both EDGE and Footprints did contact their local social services departments to inform them of this work while their projects were in progress but, at time of writing, had not received any response.

The emphasis that grew in each project on action to achieve the outcomes reflects the suggestion made in the report of Shaping Our

Lives initial research (available to download from www.shapingourlives.org.uk) that user involvement in work around outcomes must involve service users in setting and defining those outcomes.

There was an expectation when Shaping Our Lives set up these projects that they would involve some element of action but this was seen very much in terms of supporting participants to deal with issues that came up during the meetings. The full extent of the activity that has taken place, ranging from local campaigns to casework for individual users, was far beyond expectations. However, it does seem to reflect the idea in the first SOL report that:

User involvement in defining and measuring outcomes has the potential to sharpen the focus of the idea and purpose of 'user involvement'.

To some extent, this is an obvious point to be made. The literature review carried out for the initial Shaping Our Lives research noted the work of American writer Robert L. Schalock (1995) who sees outcome measurement as an essential tool in good organisational management, and user-controlled organisations benefit as much from good management as any other organisation.

However, the point goes beyond good management. It goes to the centre of what user involvement and user organisations should be seeking to achieve. This is not to say that this is not

what user-controlled organisations are doing already but that it may be useful for it to become clear and explicit that user-defined outcomes are their goal.

In the short time that they have had, the four groups in this project have been able to demonstrate the strength of this approach. Given the short time, and the limited resources available, it is reasonable to suggest that the projects have given just an initial indication of the full potential of an outcomes-based approach to user involvement.

The project has given some indicators of the approaches that work best in relation to achieving the outcomes desired by service users. The basic approach of the project through group meetings to identify collective issues and then follow up by the key worker seems to have been effective, but certainly needs more time to prove itself. Time seems to be an important factor and it is probably indicative that the greatest progress was made by the Service Users' Action Forum where there were existing relationships between the group and service providers in the area. BUG also made some progress in discussing issues with its social services department and health authority by building on previous contacts.

This would appear to show that, as well as the outcomes approach, time is needed for relationships to develop between user groups and service providers.

4 Common issues

This chapter draws out the themes that we have come across in all or in a number of the groups. Shaping Our Lives' previous projects and other research have indicated a high degree of consistency in service users' views and concerns, so it was expected that this would be reflected in this project and there would be common issues across the four groups.

The groups' efforts to address these issues resulted in some impact and positive outcomes in terms of the project's own work.

Respect for service users

They felt that the attitude of the staff at the local social services was patronising and condescending, and that they were not treated with enough respect. (BUG)

Respect for service users at an individual and collective level came up as an issue for all the projects. There were a number of clear examples of lack of respect for individual users for the groups in the project themselves: failure of the social services departments to take up the contact made by two of the projects, and the outright verbal abuse of the Service Users' Action Forum's worker when he attempted to talk to a GP about improving access to his surgery. The worker went on to succeed in changing the access to the surgery concerned.

One member complained that he was physically abused during his stay at a local mental health hospital but was not able to retaliate as he felt that he would not be believed or further abused. (Footprints)

There were also numerous examples of individual participants experiencing a lack of respect in dealings with staff. The most serious of these were experiences of physical abuse of people while staying in psychiatric hospitals and the placing of 'do not resuscitate' orders on the notes of older patients in hospital without their consent.

The Wakefield group had positive discussions on this issue which, combined with efforts at a national level in the Health Service, resulted in the agreement of local procedures about consultations that should take place before such orders are issued.

Mental health service users also saw lack of respect in terms of being made to take medication that they did not want to take, with some saying that they were ignored even when they reported serious side-effects from their drugs. They felt they were treated differently as black users when compared with their white peers in the mental health system.

They felt that, as black people, they were given higher levels of medication than their white counterparts and also that they were not offered counselling in the same way as their white counterparts. One member stated that he and a school friend went into the mental health system at about the same time and he was given medication while his friend, who was white, was given counselling and not medication. He thought this was grossly unfair. (BUG)

Other examples included users who felt that their needs were not taken seriously, particularly mental health service users who felt that their own expertise on their situation was generally ignored and that their difficulties were not properly understood by service providers. In Manchester, users of the subsidised voucher scheme for taxi travel for disabled people reported that the main taxi company often ignored their bookings. When the worker tried to take up the issue with the company, it also ignored her letters.

This lack of respect from service providers is indicative of how service users are frequently treated as second-class citizens, even by the services that are meant to support them. While the four projects are by no means a large sample, the fact that the issues have come from such diverse groups is an important addition to the growing amount of evidence on this issue. Given that three of the four groups have been run by black service users, there may also be issues around racism in the lack of respect that they have received from service providers but it has not been possible to investigate this within the scope of this project.

One of the important messages that came from Shaping Our Lives' first project was that outcomes cannot be divorced from the processes that deliver them, which challenged established thinking among academics and professionals that outcomes can be looked at without considering the process by which they are achieved. Addressing the issue of staff respect for service users is a crucial one if services are to truly support and empower service users, and deliver positive outcomes as defined by service users.

Domiciliary care

They sent out a social worker to see her but they told her they could not send anyone to do her shopping or laundry. She asked them about cleaning her home and was told that this was not essential. (EDGE)

Many of the concerns raised by participants related to the limitations of the home care services. The main complaint was around services not being allowed to undertake tasks such as window cleaning and curtain hanging. (Service Users' Action Forum)

Every group spent a considerable amount of time discussing issues around domiciliary care and it is clearly an issue of fundamental importance in users' lives.

The specific concerns varied according to the outcomes the groups wanted to attain. Participants in the two black mental health users' projects were simply concerned with being able to get a service, with people in the Footprints group particularly highlighting the lack of understanding among service providers of the importance of domiciliary services to mental health service users. Members of

BUG highlighted the outcomes of receiving assistance with keeping their homes tidy and with cooking as improving their frame of mind and motivation. Women in this group also pointed out the importance of assistance with child care.

Participants in the EDGE project were concerned about the lack of culturally sensitive services. EDGE has a service of its own which addresses exactly this issue and was able to use work on this project to increase awareness of its service. It also had contact with the local Care and Repair organisation, which provides assistance with small household maintenance jobs (e.g. dripping taps, changing light bulbs, fitting curtain rails), home safety and security, and help and advice with contacting builders and other services for larger jobs, and, again, the project has been able to increase awareness of the service.

The issue for members of the Service Users' Action Forum was lack of control over the home care service and the staff not being allowed to do certain tasks, particularly window and curtain cleaning. These concerns are to be fed into a review of the service being carried out by the social services department.

Ensuring that their home environment is clean and comfortable is clearly an important outcome for many service users across all user groups. The benefits of achieving this that were identified by participants in this project were wide ranging and likely to reduce the need to use other acute services.

Direct payments

Direct payments were discussed in each of the groups. These discussions were prompted in part by the inclusion of the Shaping Our Lives video, which features a section on direct payments, in the introductory session, but they were also raised as an issue by the project worker as they were identified as a key method for achieving user-defined outcomes in the initial project.

These discussions showed that participants had a great deal of reluctance around direct payments. They illustrated a clear need for more information and support for users who were interested in the option. For most of the participants, these meetings were the first time that they had heard of direct payments and there was particular confusion around whether the payments were part of the benefits system.

The project worker was able to explain and pass on information on direct payments. While there was recognition that they might deliver better outcomes, there remained considerable concerns about the complexities of direct payments and one of the groups included a user who had chosen to stop receiving payments because of these complexities. A representative from the National Centre for Independent Living attended one of the BUG group meetings and this did generate greater enthusiasm among some members.

This is an issue that would need to be returned to if the projects continue.

Mobility and access

After they had taken up the issue with the Highways Manager, group members were invited to take part in a survey of the city centre. Following this, there was a delay in getting a response and the files were passed to the councillor responsible for highways. As a result, the Highways Manager has informed the group that, because of the complexities of the subject and the legal rights of traders, the local authority is to appoint a dedicated Highways Enforcement Officer.
(Service Users' Action Forum)

She feels very restricted about getting out and where she can go. She wishes there were people to help her to get out and more places where she could go. She had to give up going to one day centre because they were not able to guarantee transport for her.
(EDGE)

Issues around mobility and access were raised in different contexts in each of the groups.

The Service Users' Action Forum discussed the issue in relation to a variety of services. The limited availability of the city's door-to-door transport service was criticised. Enquiries were made to find out how funding levels for the services were calculated, but it was not possible to obtain further information.

Access issues were of key importance to the group and it took up a range of issues. It liaised with the council about several problems relating to the city's pavements. These included the poor condition of some pavements, the placing of litter bins at shoulder height on lamp-posts which caused an obstruction to people with visual impairments, and the placing of signs and goods on pavements by shops and traders. The group's work in raising these issues contributed to the council appointing an officer in the highways department with specific responsibility for pavements, which should result in clear improvements in the pedestrian environment for people with mobility impairments.

The group also raised several access issues in relation to health services. These issues included improving signs at one of the local hospitals, which resulted in the simple but effective change of including the words 'blood tests' on the signs for pathology, and persuading a GP surgery to allow people with mobility impairments to be dropped off in their car park with the assistance of another agency's advice on the relevance of the Disability Discrimination Act:

Members praised the city's Ring and Ride Service. The nature of the service – picking people up from their own homes – was highly valued. Participants also praised the staff who run the service for the assistance they give to passengers. (EDGE)

EDGE endeavoured to address problems that users experienced with a subsidised taxi scheme. It also identified the positive outcomes experienced by users of Manchester's Ring and Ride door-to-door transport service for disabled people. As a result, other members of the group were given information about the service.

The Footprints group included discussion of the free use of bus and rail services provided for older and disabled people in London through the Freedom Pass. Some clarification was given on use of the pass for members of the group. BUG did not discuss mobility in detail but it was clear from ideas that came out in the 'ideal day' exercise in the introductory session that being able to get out and about was a key issue in participants' quality of life.

The importance of access and transport to the equality of disabled people is well established in the disability movement. The evidence gathered through this project illustrates the impact and importance of these issues at an individual level.

Information

The group also felt that there needed to be an improvement in the passing down of information from the professionals to users. An example given was informing users of a crisis house that nobody knew about. (BUG)

I don't think that I'm receiving the right kind of care but I don't know what to do about it. (EDGE)

Lack of information on services is a common complaint among service users and an issue that has been identified by many other projects.

EDGE found a lack of awareness on services like dial-a-ride, Care and Repair, and its own home care service.

Members of BUG were critical of the failure of service providers to give information on the support available after their initial contacts with mental health services. They said that, after initial stays in psychiatric hospitals, they were given little or no information on support services in the

community. There was a crisis house for mental health service users in the area that none of the members had heard about. In another example, it took one person almost a year after they left hospital to find out about services in the community. Even then, the information came from an informal contact. The group has suggested that an information pack should be produced for people leaving hospital and staff need to make the provision of information more of a priority.

A meeting with representatives from the social services department and the health authority confirmed that efforts were under way to improve information provision and the idea of an information pack produced by service users was discussed.

Participants in the Footprints group also noted difficulties with accessing services after leaving hospital.

The key point here is that, in many circumstances, service users cannot achieve the outcomes that they want if they are not aware of the services that are there to support them and that such a lack of information will often lead to low expectations of the outcomes that can be achieved.

Centres for users

Members of EDGE and BUG said that they found centres for service users useful:

Asked about how often she got out, she said that she went to three centres. She had to pay £4 to go to one of them, although it did not do anything for her apart from getting her out of the house. The centres were her only means of getting out of the house. She would not see anyone otherwise and felt lonely in the flat by herself. (EDGE)

The BUG group was based at a user-controlled drop-in centre so it was predictable that the participants would identify the service as valuable. As well as identifying the value of their own centre, they also looked at the wider availability of drop-in facilities and particularly the times at which they were open. Members of the group thought that the current arrangements for centres being open in the day were not adequate and that the centres would be more beneficial if they were open in the evening and first thing in the morning.

People from EDGE also identified day centres as an important part of their daily lives. Attending centres, often for meals at lunchtime, was reported as an important part of people's daily lives, particularly for older people with mobility impairments who had limited social contact. Getting to and from the centres was a problem for some of the users.

Members of the Footprints group also found day centres useful. Some complained that centres could be used only on referral from a social worker or psychiatrist and wanted to be able to 'self-refer'.

5 Problems and challenges

Shaping Our Lives' experience of carrying out a project by working through four diverse and independent user groups has not always been easy. In many ways, this project has been based on the antithesis of what would normally be considered to be good practice in user involvement, in that an idea that has been developed at a national level has been implemented by a national organisation at a local level, and this may have been at the root of some of these problems.

The key difference between this and other similar situations is that Shaping Our Lives is a national user-controlled organisation, though this by no means meant that the four local groups had to put aside their existing work and priorities to be a part of Shaping Our Lives' work. It has meant that it has been difficult to ensure that the work has happened within the allotted timeframe.

There have also been several other problems and challenges across the project as a whole that need to be recorded in this report. The first of these problems related to external factors that make life in general very difficult for all local user organisations but the other problems relate to this project and point to some important lessons that need to be addressed in any future work.

General difficulties facing local user organisations

Research by the National Centre for Independent Living, the British Council of Disabled People and the Disability Research Unit at the University of Leeds (Barnes *et al.*, 2000) has highlighted the precarious situation of many service user organisations. The experience of this project has highlighted some of these problems.

All the projects were based with groups with very limited staffing. This caused particular problems with two of the groups when the co-ordinators had to be absent from work for extended periods. In many ways, the project was fortunate not to experience greater difficulty in this area.

These issues may also be evident in the fact that three other groups that had expressed an interest in taking part in the project were not able to pursue the interest.

Time and resources

It has been noted above that the Service Users' Action Forum's approach to holding meetings more frequently worked very effectively. Other groups also identified a desire to hold more frequent meetings and most of the groups wanted to involve more service users as the work progressed. Limited resources meant that this was not possible within the current project.

All the workers also reported the need to spend more time on the project than had initially been anticipated during the planning of the work. The experience of having carried out these four projects should give Shaping Our Lives a much more realistic basis for planning similar work in the future.

Producing the evidence of outcomes

Looking at the project as a whole and the reports that have come out of the four individual projects, the actual evidence that has come out of the individual projects has not been as strong as it could have been.

This is probably an issue that should have been addressed more explicitly at the outset of the project with more discussions with the key workers/co-ordinators about how the group meetings should be recorded and written up in order to ensure that the results of the work were as useful as possible.

A key part of any future work should be some training on research skills for the key workers. Again, this is an important lesson that needed to be learnt by actually carrying out these development projects.

6 Findings

Findings on work on outcomes

The key purpose of this project was to examine the process of service users being involved in work on outcomes at a local level.

1 In each project, the approach of looking at outcomes from users' perspectives has led to action being taken by the groups to influence those outcomes. This indicates that user-led work on outcomes needs to include scope for action – rather than being carried out simply in order to monitor and evaluate outcomes. This supports the finding in SOL's initial project that involving users in work on outcomes must include users in defining the outcomes.

2 Point one above means that work to support users to examine outcomes is more intensive than originally anticipated. All of the workers reported that the work took more time than expected.

3 Also following from point one is the issue around frequency of meetings. The initial approach – looking at outcomes as a way of monitoring and evaluating services – indicated that gaps of around six months between meetings would be appropriate. With the emphasis that emerged on action, more frequent meetings became more appropriate. The Service Users' Action Forum's more frequent meetings have certainly given it a greater degree of momentum than the other groups, and the Footprints group expressed a desire to meet more often than had been planned for. Future work would need to take this into account and the gap between meetings needs to be shortened.

4 More consideration needed to be given to skills required by the workers and participants in the groups. There is a particular need for research skills to ensure that evidence of outcomes experienced by service users is gathered and recorded as effectively as possible.

5 As with Shaping Our Lives' initial project, this project has shown that service users are like anyone else in looking at their lives as a whole when considering outcomes. The project has covered issues relating to social and health care services, transport, access and the built environment, employment and training, and income and benefits. While this is a strength for the work, it may also cause problems for securing funding as it may not fit into 'boxes' as easily as local funders would like.

Findings on outcomes for service users

While this project was primarily about the process of involving service users in outcomes, it was designed as a real exercise with practical outcomes for the groups and individuals involved. The four projects have used their results to inform the work of local service providers and there are also a number of key messages that can be drawn from the common themes that emerged across the four groups.

These are as follows.

1 Respect for services: participants in the groups gave examples of their experiences of being treated without respect by service providers. The groups themselves provided further evidence of this, with social services departments failing to respond to approaches from two of the groups.

2 Domiciliary care and having a clean and tidy home environment is important to the majority of service users. Support to achieve this outcome can have a significant wider impact on the quality of life of service users.

3 Direct payments: members of the groups were interested in direct payments but had some reservations about how they would work in practice. Further information and support is required.

4 Mobility and access: users placed considerable importance on being able to get around and to access facilities but continue to experience difficulties in both areas.

5 Information: most of the groups had discussions on the difficulties of getting information about services and the inevitable difficulties that this led to in obtaining services.

6 Centres for users: participants valued having access to drop-in and day centres but they were keen for them to be more flexible and open to them when they most required support, such as in the evenings.

Beyond these findings, perhaps the most important achievement of the project has been the personal benefit that individual participants have gained from being involved in the work. Participants have said that the project has made them feel valued and have expressed strong enthusiasm for the work, as evidenced in the attendance records for all the groups.

This group has really helped me to speak up. At my recent appointment with my psychiatrist, I asked to see my records and noticed that some of the information on my records was incorrect, and asked that such information be removed. The psychiatrist tried to dismiss my challenge but then had to agree with me as his explanation as to how this information was obtained lacked evidence. He tried to explain that this information was given to him but every time he tried to make me withdraw my demand for corrections I was more determined that my records should be corrected. In the end he agreed, but I will make sure that I see the corrections when I next go to see him. (Footprints)

This should be seen as a result in itself for the project, and an important result given the growing evidence of users feeling disenchanted with being 'researched'. Any research project that leaves its participants feeling valued and enthusiastic for the

work has done at least one thing right.

As well as being a result of its own value, this should also be seen as another indicator of the value of an outcomes-based approach to user involvement. The approach puts the individual service user and their views, needs and wishes at the centre of the work, as they should be. Re-establishing this as the purpose and principle of user involvement may be essential at a time when many service users have become disillusioned and disenchanted with the idea.

The conclusion of this project comes at an opportune time. The later part of 2001 saw the new national bodies for improving quality and standards in social care starting to come into operation. At the same time, the move towards closer working between health and social care services, particularly through primary care trusts, has been gathering pace.

Against this background, the need to refocus and revitalise user involvement through the use of the outcomes perspective is both timely and important. This project is a small start for such a major change. Shaping Our Lives is in the process of establishing a national network of organisations controlled by service users and this will provide a framework in which to develop this approach.

Beyond this, there is a need for further project work to build on the work carried out by this project, and particularly to support the continuation of the four groups that formed this project. These groups have achieved a substantial amount in a very short time and with very little resources, and in many ways this first year is best seen as a pilot phase for a project that would continue this work over a more substantial period of time.

This would enable Shaping Our Lives to fully develop and assess this approach to service users working on outcomes.

One of the clearest messages to come from this project has been the need for increased time and resources for the work to be carried out as effectively as possible, and in particular to support more frequent meetings and to enable more people to be involved.

SOL will develop a proposal for a new project that will support the continuation of the existing groups at an expanded level in accordance with the findings of this project. The new project would also carry out local and national dissemination about the work to service users and service providers.

The national dissemination would need to form part of a national strategy that Shaping Our Lives would need to develop to promote this type of work among user groups.

The possible combination of this further project with the establishment of the Shaping Our Lives National User Network during 2002 gives the potential for the beginnings of real movement towards linking user involvement and outcomes.

PART II
THE REPORTS OF THE FOUR LOCAL GROUPS

7 Black User Group

Introduction

We were asked to take part in Shaping Our Lives' research into user-defined outcomes – what users wanted from the services and what they were getting, were they satisfied and how could things be improved.

The project began in November 2000. The group of ten black mental health service users met every six to eight weeks mainly at the Black Cafe, a centre for black users.

Over the year, the group was to discuss issues pertaining to users and especially black users. We had five sessions over the year.

A day in the life

In the first session, the group was encouraged to talk about a typical day in their lives and issues that they thought were important to users.

The typical day was not unusual; users generally got up between 10.00 and 12.00 in the day. Some would have breakfast but quite often they would not, as they could not make the effort. Then they would do things like go to a day centre, or an appointment. Two users had to take their children to school and that would take up the morning, then they would go on to a centre.

During the day, people would make phone calls and see friends, and eat and go to the pub. One user had to have a nurse come round in the day to dress his wounds. Users stated that they wanted many more benefits so that they could do the things that they wanted to do. They would also spend the day doing housework or going to the gym. Users felt that it was important to be occupied in the day. Those with children felt that they would like help with the children, someone to collect the children from school and someone to help with cooking them an evening meal. Users felt that, if they had someone to collect the children from school, then they could spend longer at a day centre. None of the users felt that their day was a waste.

Some of the users had a lot of help from their families; this help would be to cook meals for them or assistance with housework. Users felt that they fared better in a clean and tidy environment, and housework and cleanliness were very important to the majority of them. Most of the group felt that they needed the help of a support worker in the evenings.

An ideal day

The second session was spent talking mainly about an ideal typical day, what sort of day the users would like to have if they could. In this session, people talked about going to the pub again, going to see a football match, having a meal cooked by someone in their family – either their mum or a nephew or niece – just going out to a mate's house.

Interestingly enough, most users specified a wish to get up early in the morning, the most favourite time being around 7.00 or 8.00 a.m. Upon rising early, it was also their wish to have a good breakfast. Users also wanted help with the housework and cooking, and in their ideal day this was available to them. They also wanted an evening service open for black people. In their ideal day, some users wanted to do quite ordinary things like spend the evening with a few friends playing music. Parents in the group wanted parenting classes and a nanny to help with very small children and assistance with the evening meal. They also wanted someone to look after the children while they attended a day centre. One user would like a t'ai chi teacher early in the morning and another would like to go jogging. Users wanted to work if possible and study, and they were able to do this in an ideal day. They were also much fitter from going to the gym. They also wanted to be up to date with events by reading the newspapers and going to college to learn computing and other modern skills. Users also wanted to be involved politically with issues of the day. In some users' ideal day, they were provided with reading and writing groups and resources that offered gym and sports facilities. Some members of the group talked about the state of where they lived and how they would like it to be in an ideal situation. Most users would like to enjoy a clean environment with equipment that worked to keep their places free from dirt. One user stated that she would like a hoover with carpet-washing facilities on it to keep the carpet clean.

A few users would like to be without their medication or to be on less of it. Members of the group stated that they wanted more user-led organisations and resources. Time and time again, they wanted more money from their benefits so they could do things like go shopping, buy a takeaway, go out clubbing, take a day trip away somewhere, go on a course, pay for crèches, have driving lessons. Their ideal typical day would also include things like going to London Zoo, or a sports centre, or museums and places relating to art. Members also said that the holiday scheme should pay for holidays abroad as a week away in the country costing around £400 is the same as the average fare to the West Indies and users felt that a holiday there would be of far more benefit to them than a holiday here.

In conclusion, when we looked at the typical day and the ideal typical day, we found that there was not much difference. In both days, users wanted to eat, they wanted someone to cook for them and help with housework, and they wanted to be able to go out with their friends and go to the pub. Overall, users felt that the main obstacle stopping them from carrying out the things they wanted to do was not enough benefits and no support in their areas of need.

Experiences of services

Other issues that came up were what users thought about the services. They felt that the attitude of the staff at the local social services was patronising and condescending, and that they were not treated with enough respect. People felt as though they were not listened to and that professionals ran things by the book too much. They also felt that their own expertise on mental illness should be utilised as they were living the illness.

Users thought that there was not enough understanding of the illness that they had. As it was an invisible illness, they felt that it was not taken seriously enough unless you did something drastic when you said that you were ill. People said that they were only taken into hospital when a professional like a social worker or Community Psychiatric Nurse (CPN) went with them to the hospital and verified that they were ill. They said that this was not good enough as professionals only got involved when you had done something seriously wrong. People wanted more notice taken of them because they felt they were not so mad as not to know when they were ill.

Members of the group did not comment much on their stay in hospital but it was said that the Patients' Charter was not applicable once you had left hospital. The group felt that, after their stay in hospital, the service was not good enough. People were not told of services that were available and were left to their own devices as to how to get follow-up services after they had left hospital. One member was left for one year after a stay in hospital before follow-up services were available to him. It was his GP – someone outside of the mental health system – who eventually put him in touch with mental health follow-up services. He was very unhappy about this, even though to date his circumstances had changed positively. The group suggested that an information pack be devised and given to people leaving hospital. This information pack would tell people how to access services, and where to go and who to see. The group also felt that there needed to be an improvement in the passing down of information from the professionals to users. An example given was informing users of a crisis house that nobody knew about.

Users also felt that care in the community was not working. Unless they accessed the services themselves, they felt that they were easily forgotten. For care in the community to work, there needed to be more social workers readily available and at the moment this was not the case. Users felt that it should not be so hard to get a social worker. They felt that more effort should be put into preventative methods of treatment rather than treating illnesses when they got very serious. This would cut down on hospital admissions and improve the quality of life of users.

People said that, once they were out of hospital, they were not told about benefits available to them and that they found things out through word of mouth. Parents in the group felt that the fact that they had children was not taken into account. They wanted crèches available to them when they went to visit day centres, as quite often they could not attend centres because they had nowhere to put the children and no one to look after them while they were there.

Users felt that there was a gross lack of communication between professionals. Although there had been an integration of the services, sometimes things that were in their file and needed to be passed on to the relevant parties were not passed on; one user in the group had experience of this. The group also felt that users should have a crisis card so that, if they were in a crisis, people dealing with them would find the card and know who to contact. Members of the group felt that staff changed too frequently not giving them a chance to build up a relationship or, if they built a relationship, the member of staff would leave soon after, so they would have to start all over again with someone new. People did not like having to repeat their story over and over again to different individuals. They felt that, with frequent staff changes, their care was affected. They thought that the building of a relationship was important as staff who were familiar with your case were likely to know better how to handle it and this could only

lead to an improvement in your care.

Members of the group complained that they thought they were being used as guinea pigs for doctors. Quite often, they would go to their doctor with a complaint and the doctor would suggest a new medication that had recently come out onto the market. People did not like the idea of being used to try out new drugs. This was a common point in the group and members felt strongly about it. They had the opinion that they were being used as stepping stones in the careers of professionals. They felt that professionals came into mental health for a few years, worked with people at the grass-roots level, then used the experience to further their careers and did not really care about the users that got them that promotion. An even worse scenario was people who came into mental health with no intention of staying and who saw users simply as a means to an end in furthering their careers.

The group also talked about medication. They felt that, as black people, they were given higher levels of medication than their white counterparts and also that they were not offered counselling in the same way as their white counterparts. One member stated that he and a schoolfriend went into the mental health system at about the same time and he was given medication while his friend, who was white, was given counselling and not medication. He thought this was grossly unfair. It was believed by the group that white professionals were of the opinion that black people could not cope with counselling and were therefore not given it. The professional view was that black people with mental health problems were wild, violent and dangerous and therefore needed to be given higher levels of medication than their white counterparts. This problem was especially true of black men. The group also generally felt that, if they were to be given counselling, they would like it from someone who was culturally the same as them as a fellow black person would more easily understand the problems of another black person. Some members of the group felt that there were issues about life that they could not explain to a white person and would be uncomfortable trying to do so. The group pointed out that psychology books were written by Europeans with Europeans in mind. They also pointed out that Afro-Caribbeans and Africans and other blacks were different, had different cultures and experiences, and saw life in a different light. At present, the services do not reflect this. The group felt that the black voice was ignored and that, as users, they wanted more power. They would like some kind of drop-in service for black people, which was open in the evening – somewhere where they could 'chill out' and relax, with food, music, TV and video available. They wanted this place to be user led. They felt that they were capable of running such a service and would need a professional there only to satisfy any legal requirements. Members of the group also wanted to see gyms in hospital as a regular feature. There was one in St Bernard's in Ealing and people felt that the use of it contributed positively to their recovery. They said that, if they were stuck in hospital with nothing to do, they would use the gym if they were given the chance – especially if they could be motivated to go.

Although members of the group were critical of the present services, it was not discussed in detail what they would prefer. Direct payments was talked about after the group had seen a video on it and had received a visit from a representative of the National Centre for Independent Living. Some group members felt that it might help with the child-care situation and others felt that it might help them now that they had started work. Employment rules were discussed and people were inquisitive but there is still reluctance in the group as no one has taken it up.

Summary and conclusion

The project has shown through the many issues discussed that the relationship between professionals and users, especially black users,

needs to be improved. The members of the group felt that they were not respected and were even ignored, and they wanted improvements in consultations with them. They felt that the black voice was unheard and that services did not reflect the large numbers of black people in the mental health system. There was quite a lot of pessimism in the group about how and when things would change. The group believed that the main thing that needed to change was people's attitudes and that this would take years.

The exercise of writing about your typical day and ideal typical day threw light on the fact that users did not want to do anything too much out of the ordinary and yet they were not able to do what they wanted to do. This indicates a gap in the services that perhaps direct payments could fill. However, people did not feel comfortable going to social services to arrange this, which was possibly one reason for the reluctance to take up direct payments.

Users said that they needed more support and that this should come from more listening to users. They felt that their 'invisible illness' was still not properly understood. More communication was necessary and improved communication between users and professionals and between professionals themselves. Parents within the mental health system said they needed more support and somewhere to put their children with someone to look after them while they were at day centres.

Members of the group felt that they were only taken notice of when they were ill and needed to go into hospital. It was not acknowledged that they themselves knew when they were ill – it always had to be a professional that got them into hospital. Care in hospitals was not really discussed in detail but users said that they wanted gyms in hospital as they felt exercise helped them to recover. It was also felt that more emphasis should be put into preventative methods of treatment, although what these methods should be was not discussed.

Medication was a strong issue and people felt

that they were being treated like guinea pigs. Quite a few of these medications are dangerous to take and users did not like this. A meeting was arranged after the five sessions and at the end of the year with the assistant director of services, Heather Schroeder, and the head of adult acute services, Trevor Farmer. Issues that the group had been discussing throughout the year were brought up. A lot of the issues that users had been talking about were already in progress, for example the crisis card, but matters like staff retention were said to be an ongoing problem. It was reported that there was an exercise area in the new mental health block at Charing Cross. Heather Schroeder and Trevor Farmer said they would look into the issue of black users getting counselling as they were concerned with the view on that. They also said that finances dictated a lot of what could and could not be done but on the whole we were listened to and the meeting went positively. This is to be reported back to the group.

To conclude, I think it has to be said that the group is generally unsatisfied with the way things are at present. Although there is a shake up in the mental health system with the implementations of the recommendations of the National Service Framework (NSF), a lot still has to be done. Hopefully, in the next year, we can look at possible solutions to the problems that have arisen in the last year.

8 Footprints (UK) and Waltham Forest Black Mental Health Service User Group

Introduction

The *first phase* of the initial project organised by Shaping Our Lives was centred on a series of focus group meetings with a number of user groups who worked on looking at the concept of outcomes and the different experiences in their individual lives.

Footprints (UK) was subsequently invited to participate in the *second phase* of the project in taking forward the concept of outcomes.

A black user group, Down to Earth, an independent black user group but based in the same premises as Waltham Forest Black People Mental Health Association, was selected to work in partnership with Footprints (UK).

Population profile of Waltham Forest

Waltham Forest is composed of a diverse mix of people with pockets of deprivation more prominent throughout the borough. Table 1 reflects the population based on the 1991 census.

Table 1 Population profile of Waltham Forest

	% of total population
Black African	8
Black Afro-Caribbean	5.2
Black Other	2.6
Indian	4.0
Pakistani	9.1
Bangladeshi	1.1
Chinese	0.7
Other Asian	2.1
Other ethnic groups	3.1
White	64.2

Note: overall population = 220,818.

The process

An introductory meeting was held in June 2000 to meet with members of the user group and to seek their co-operation in participating in the project.

Participants were given a brief overview of the objectives of the group, explaining how their participation could impact on their personal development and increase their awareness of issues that affect their lives within a mental health context.

It was also important to use the session to enable participants to familiarise themselves with some of the language/jargon being used such as 'outcomes', 'concepts', 'independent living', etc. as many experienced difficulties in discussing the provision and quality of services in these terms.

The follow-up session focused on the showing of a video where users gave their testimonies and views as to what it was like to work around outcomes, and how they were able to familiarise themselves with the jargon and increase their awareness of the different benefits available to them. The video also showed users expressing the importance of being confident and being able to assert themselves in ensuring that their needs and rights were met.

The first session was in June 2000 and the last session (evaluation) was held in February 2002. It was felt that this was necessary to ascertain whether or not the sessions were of benefit to them and whether the group's interest and motivation were being maintained; also to find out how many members wished to continue to participate in the group.

A total of 31 members registered for the project. As the sessions progressed, the attendance increased with average attendance of 20. A total of seven sessions were held including the introductory and evaluation meetings, with the overall attendance totalling 140.

Key findings

- Mental health services provided to service users should be monitored in terms of ethnicity, disability and gender. These details should then be published.

- Services should also be monitored in terms of users' satisfaction and outcome of services provided, and service users should play a role in such evaluation.

- Service users should be trained prior to being invited to participate in decision-making forums such as steering groups, etc.

- Lack of response from health trusts and social services in the project: members felt that this clearly demonstrated the lack of recognition/ respect shown by policy-makers – this indicated how black users are treated by professionals.

- A need to have a full-time worker to work with other black service users – especially those who do not attend day centres – in terms of capacity building.

- There is an urgent need for social workers' performance to be closely monitored as the quality of service received from some is poor. If users were to complain, they feared that they would be victimised as professionals protect each other. One member complained that he was physically abused during his stay at a local mental health hospital but was not able to retaliate as he felt that he would not be believed or would be further abused.

- There is an urgent need for an independent mental health advocacy service as many black users are not listened to or respected as human beings.

- There is also a need for an information pack to be available for users experiencing mental health problems.

- Visit other user groups to enhance their networking skills.

- Workshops to be organised to improve skills of members such as facilitating meetings, minute taking, drafting agendas and public speaking.

Key outcomes

- The majority of participants expressed their increased level of motivation and confidence in issues that affect their lives, and being able to take on the authorities in challenging practitioners. For example, one member of the group gave a testimony of how, as a result of her increased knowledge and awareness, she was able to ask her psychiatrist to see her records:

This group has really helped me to speak up. At my recent appointment with my psychiatrist, I asked to see my records and noticed that some of the information on my records was incorrect, and asked that such information be removed. The psychiatrist tried to dismiss my challenge but then had to agree with me as his explanation as to how this information was obtained lacked evidence. He tried to explain that this information was given to him but every time he tried to make me withdraw my demand for corrections I was more determined that my records should be corrected. In the end he agreed, but I will make sure that I see the corrections when I next go to see him.

- A total of 15 members indicated an interest in learning/developing their computer skills – as a result a successful joint funding bid for the total of £5,000 was made to the Awards for All scheme run by the Community Fund. The course commenced on 18 February 2002 and ran for ten weeks. It was very successful and we are now looking for training for other members of the group.

- Participants are now more relaxed and open in sharing with other members of the group their thoughts about mental health issues and their personal strategies for coping with mental health problems.

Possible areas of work for the future

The project was relatively short and has really been the start of what needs to be an ongoing process. A number of areas of work were identified for the future.

- Funding to be sought to provide a video on group activities, ideas and areas of concern – it is expected that this video can be used as a learning tool for other user groups.

- Organise workshops on different aspects of mental health, e.g. coping strategies and recognising when one is becoming unwell. Members would like to share their experiences with a wider group.

- Invite psychiatrists and social workers to talk about their work.

- Publish a booklet for local service users.

- Training workshop sessions to focus on volunteering – this is seen as a form of preparation for future employment.

Monitoring and evaluation

Thirty-one members registered for the project – 21 female and ten male. In terms of attendance at the sessions, it was 70 per cent female, 30 per cent male.

There were seven sessions with an average attendance of 30 people.

The ethnic breakdown of the participants was 96 per cent African and African/Caribbean origin, 1 per cent Asian and 1 per cent Turkish.

Three of the participants were refugees.

What worked and did not work

This was a new area of work and we needed to look at what would and would not work.

Areas that worked well were as follows.

- Having an introductory session prior to the actual start of the session in order to familiarise members with the facilitator (concepts and language to be used), to get members used to sharing thoughts with each other, to build trust within the group.

- Ground-rules, e.g. confidentiality, respect for each other's views, commitment to group in terms of attendance, etc., the dos and don'ts of participating in meetings where different members can feel safe in their participation.

- Working with participants already known to the facilitator enables participants to relax and have confidence in the group – building a sense of belonging and trust of the abilities of the facilitator.

- Financial incentive – a sense of valuing their contribution – by sharing their experiences and ideas to influence change.

- Participants experiencing actual outcomes from their discussions, e.g. funding for computer classes acts as a motivation that it is not all talk and no action. This is viewed to be a practical example of the fact that their ideas and suggestions can make a difference.

- Cohesion of group: participants taking part equally, each being given an opportunity to share and express their individual views and valuing each other. Views: realising that individuals are not the only ones experiencing mental health problems.

- Facilitator being sensitive and flexible in facilitating the group while at the same time focusing on the objectives of the session. It is important not to be too set in their own agenda, but to be guided by what the group wants to discuss.

- Working in partnership with the 'Shaping Our Lives' development worker, especially at meetings and submitting joint bids. It is important to maintain a joint approach.

- Attending advisory group meetings for the project as a whole – sharing and building knowledge of what other groups are doing in their own localities. It is important that at least two member representatives are nominated by the group to attend and report back from each meeting. This enables the group to be aware of issues raised in a wider forum.

Areas in which there were problems or that did not work were as follows.

- Insufficient funds for facilitator and administrative costs, facilitating and travelling, etc. In practice, the budget did not reflect the amount of work that was entailed in carrying out the project. A lot of good will was shown in terms of follow-up time, organising meetings and attending advisory group meetings.

- Too long a gap between meetings taking place: once members are motivated it is important that the motivation is maintained so that members do not lose interest or view the meetings as having no focus or serious approach to the issues. It is important to maintain bonding among members.

- Lack of a clear decision on the future of the project – exit strategy – where do we go after the project is completed?

Conclusion

In conclusion, it was really encouraging to have worked with a group of people who clearly expressed the benefits gained from participating in the 'Shaping Our Lives' project.

It was encouraging also because members of the group demonstrated their commitment to establish and take ownership of the group as the session progressed. The introduction of new ideas and strategies in functioning as a group helped to attract new members.

It is, nonetheless, disappointing that the group did not receive a response to their invitation to Waltham Forest Health Trust or Social Services to take an interest in the outcomes from the group. This, I believe, clearly shows the disrespect or lack of seriousness with which policy-makers view the opinions of black mental health users.

As mentioned above, it was disappointing to learn of the abuse of power that some practitioners have shown to certain members of the group; further, of the poor quality of social workers who are employed and allocated to provide services to such a vulnerable and discriminated against group of clients.

On the whole, I believe that the project was successful in the sense that changes in attitudes, confidence and awareness were clearly evident during the evaluation. In fact, psychiatrists are now being monitored and challenged in a positive way in terms of accuracy of information on their records.

9 Service Users' Action Forum

Background

The Wakefield project arose from research by Shaping Our Lives, which was interested in the development of work looking at the outcomes of health and community care services for service users.

The project recognised that providers consider outcomes as a means of monitoring how good services are. It was decided that the work would be completed through groups to consider the outcomes experienced by service users, whether those outcomes were as wanted and to lobby the appropriate authorities if not.

Aims of the development project

The following aims were developed.

- Involve service users in defining and measuring outcomes over an extended period.

- Have an input into and influence services in the areas where the project operates.

- Enable participants in the project to improve their situations through the consideration of outcomes.

- Develop models of good practice for service users to take the lead in the discussions on outcomes.

Specific objectives were developed for the Wakefield project group that reflected the input of older people.

Methodology

Two methods were employed for the feedback of information about the outcome of services:

- the completion of a diary by participants, based on the diary method used in a previous project, the Talk-back Project, to record their own experiences to feed back to the meetings

- discussion at the meetings of participants' experiences of service outcomes.

The meetings were held bi-monthly with the average number of participants being eight at each meeting. There were also personal visits to those participants who were unable to attend meetings. The first meeting took place in September 2000 and the last in July 2001.

Particular concerns about a participant's poor experience of in-patient care were dealt with during the time of the project following the completion of a detailed report, which was passed to the appropriate trust officials for action.

Service outcomes identified

Information received from the project's participants about their concerns, and their positive experiences, showed the broad range of issues of concern to older people.

A wide-range of positive experiences/outcomes were identified, as follows.

1 Sheltered accommodation:
   - feeling 'not alone, but independent'
   - a good transitory option
   - relocation: welcomed and pleased with new home
   - social activities available
   - security
   - council relocation correspondence was clear and understandable
   - committed warden
   - high standards
   - easy access to transport and amenities.

2 Transport:
   - access bus trips to supermarket welcomed.

3 Health:
- NHS Walk-in Centre made immediate referral to A&E
- better discharge arrangements negotiated by family
- NHS Walk-in Centre good care
- care received on P ward lovely (Elderly Care).

4 Aids and adaptations:
- adaptations completed for discharge.

5 Home help:
- very good.

The project also looked at areas where participants had experienced difficulties/negative outcomes. The following is a list of all of the topics that were raised in this context.

1 Aids and adaptations:
- need for walk-in shower – not provided because of house/cost.

2 Meals on wheels:
- concern at lack of choice and quality.

3 Sheltered accommodation:
- lack of consultation regarding refurbishment plans
- wardens being allowed to do odd jobs
- no help with relocation/no provision of boxes
- relocation: no help with taking down/ putting up
- need for temporary parking permits
- need for Carelink pull cords in lounge/ kitchen
- no signs to entrance to sheltered housing complex
- problem of disposing of boxes after move
- poor location of fridge power point
- difficulties using communal clothes-washing facilities
- no shower available.

4 Home care services:
- need for help with floor cleaning
- reliable private home help/occasional help
- need for help with spring cleaning
- need for help with hanging curtains
- inappropriate dress
- difficulties with shopping.

5 Health:
- concern with notes marked 'do not resuscitate'
- concern at impersonal approach of doctors
- no help with stopping smoking
- blood pressure monitoring
- access to health services – waiting times at GP's
- access to health services – waiting times for appointments with consultants
- problems of miscommunication in GP's surgery
- communication problems with foreign GPs
- no access to hospital transport because of criteria
- medical records not available to Walk-in Centre
- Walk-in Centre prescription concerns
- unable to gain access to GP's entrance from taxi
- waiting times for chiropody appointment
- problems of delayed discharge
- waiting for beds for surgery
- ear problem dealt with without examination
- need for appropriate signing for blood tests at hospital
- need for clarification for process of test results
- lack of public toilets at Pinderfields General Hospital
- no treatment from GP – no access to treatment room
- over 75 health checks by GPs not being compulsory
- changed medication without explanation

- delay in changes to repeat prescriptions
- not informed of ward transfer of relative
- non-completion of scan although consent given
- medication not transferred resulting in recurring problem
- concern at lack of help with feeding/ drinking on wards
- private health care – confusion over payment of account
- misinformation about withdrawal of services
- poor care on general ward
- non-transfer of notes, resulting in delay for consultation
- insensitive, inappropriate consultation
- illness not identified on general ward
- volunteers not trained in leading for visually impaired
- care at home because of concern about wait in hospital.

6 Transport:
- concessionary fares only from 9.30 a.m. to 3.00 p.m.
- lack of services on Sunday
- transport to hospital – no reimbursement for taxi
- no transport for residents relocating in sheltered housing.

7 Highways and pathways:
- poor condition of pavements around Town Hall
- litter bins dangerous for those with impaired vision
- crossing points without signals for the visually impaired
- work on pavements causing obstruction
- obstruction caused by 'A' boards
- obstruction caused by cars on pavements.

Analysis of negative outcomes and action taken

Health

Analysing the information received, it is clear that a major concern is waiting times, either for GP or hospital services. Such waiting time concerns include problems encountered with delayed discharge, anxieties around the uncertainties of the availability of beds for surgery and the frustration of waiting for consultation appointments. Indeed, one participant had a fall at home but was advised not to attend hospital because of waiting times. They were cared for at home by family members and the GP.

During the project, concerns were also expressed about the standards of care on general wards. One incident was raised separately with officials from the acute trust and other difficulties were encountered, from the non-transfer of medication, to concerns about the lack of help for feeding and drinking.

Action was taken on a number of the issues identified.

- *'Do not resuscitate' orders*: participants' concerns over this issue led to discussions being held between the project and the acute trust. Subsequently, the trust undertook work to develop protocols to ensure consultation prior to a 'do not resuscitate' order, which gave participants considerable reassurance.

- *Access to GP's surgery*: there was a positive outcome to the matter of access to a GP's surgery, where a barrier had been placed that prevented patients being dropped off at the entrance by vehicle. The matter was raised with the Practice Manager, but the reply was less than satisfactory. The matter was passed to the Disability Advice Officer at DIAL (Disability Information and Advice Line), which has resulted in access now being available on request. The barrier will be lifted to allow those patients who need to alight at the door.

- *NHS Walk-in Centre*: a group member raised a concern that, following a visit to the Centre, she had been prescribed medication which, when checked, was found to be dangerous to take in conjunction with other medication which she was taking. The matter was flagged up to the Centre and the health authority. Guidance appears to have been given on this issue – when another participant visited the centre at a later date, he was asked about medication that he was taking before being prescribed further medicine. There were also positive experiences of the care received, including an immediate referral to A&E.

Sheltered accommodation

One participant experienced many of the problems relating to a move necessitated by refurbishment requirements. Most of the problems were similar to those encountered by many older people, who often find it hard to do odd jobs, such as the putting up and taking down of household items, and would welcome reliable help.

However, those participants living in sheltered accommodation were generally pleased with their homes. Security related to the sense of not being alone, but being able to live independently, was perceived as a major strength.

One participant moved to a new sheltered flat during the course of the meetings. She reported how this had had a positive impact on her quality of life:

Since moving my life has run smoothly. Easy access to transport and all amenities has greatly improved my quality of life.

She noted that the standards in the new flat are higher and the warden is 'committed and

professional'. She also observed that differences in standards are often to do with having the right staff in the right job.

Home care services

Many of the concerns raised by participants related to the limitations of the home care services. The main complaint was around services not being allowed to undertake tasks such as window cleaning and curtain hanging.

Information was also obtained about the London Borough of Lewisham's provision of a spring cleaning service. This information was passed to the new Director of Housing and Social Care in Wakefield, from whom a positive response was received. The new Director has instigated a review of home care services, which should be completed in six months, and members of the project will be invited to contribute to the discussions.

Highways and pathways

Problems were encountered by one participant in particular in the area around the venue where the project meetings took place. The problems included the poor state of the pavements and the situation of bins at shoulder height, which were a particular hazard for those with a visual impairment.

The proliferation of 'A' boards and display baskets outside shops was also raised.

After they had taken up the issue with the Highways Manager, group members were invited to take part in a survey of the city centre. Following this, there was a delay in getting a response and the files were passed to the councillor responsible for highways.

As a result, the Highways Manager has informed the group that, because of the complexities of the subject and the legal rights of traders, the local authority is to appoint a dedicated Highways Enforcement Officer.

Conclusion

The feedback from the participants of the project can be taken as a 'snapshot' in time and reflects many issues of national and local concern.

In the health arena, concerns with waiting times predominate, at best creating frustration, at worst causing one participant to reconsider hospital care. Support for independent living is shown to be a further concern. Local home care services have been found to be limited and there is frustration for older people unable to complete odd jobs, such as curtain hanging and changing light bulbs.

In introducing the idea of outcomes, the project did enable participants to think about the outcomes they wanted in their lives and the support they needed to achieve them, and it started to address how to deliver those outcomes with relevant service providers.

10 Ethnic Disabled Group Emerged (EDGE)

Introduction

This report describes the work carried out by EDGE with Shaping Our Lives between October 2000 and September 2001.

The project was set up for one year to support individuals to look at and reflect on their lives and the outcomes that they experience. It included seminars, home visits and meetings with other organisations.

The work took EDGE to a different level in the way it looks at the problems of ethnic disabled people. It matched EDGE's existing objectives of:

- assisting ethnic disabled people to access voluntary and statutory services

- developing partnerships between ethnic disabled people and statutory/voluntary services.

What the project did

The activities carried out for the project were challenging, eventful and very fulfilling.

The project was due to start in October 2000. At first it was slow to take off because of some administrative problems and getting the information out to members. When things did get moving, it was encouraging to see the enormous interest in the project. With more resources, the project could have started working with 80 people at the start; by the end, the number might have gone as high as 250 people because of the level of interest generated by contact with a range of organisations.

During the course of the project, EDGE was in contact with:

- Moss Side and Hulme Women's Action Forum

- Manchester Action Forum for the Health Care of Ethnic Minorities

- Moss Side and Hulme Task Force

- Black Disabled People Group

- Bibini Y6 Carers' Group for Ethnic Disabled People

- Afro-Caribbean Care Group

- African Society

- Afro-Caribbean Mental Health

- Social Services

- Greater Manchester Coalition of Disabled People

- Moss Side Job Centre

- Moss Side Leisure Centre

- Manchester Sickle Cell Centre

- Manchester Mini Bus Agency

- Ring and Ride

- Ebony Homecare Services

- Voluntary Action Manchester

- Greenhays Education Centre

- Adult Education Centre.

The project was carried out with a combination of meetings and seminars with groups, as outlined in the original project plan, and one-to-one work and support by the development worker. This was because we found that ethnic disabled people preferred to talk about their lives on a one-to-one basis rather than in a group. Home visits were made to all participants during the course of the project. This was also important as some members were unable to attend the seminars because of disabilities that limited their mobility and these people would have been excluded if the project had been based around just seminars.

The visits seemed to be very welcome but they did take a lot of time. On average, the time spent on each visit was two to three hours. Some members had serious problems that required the worker to spend a considerable amount of time with them and to carry out a lot of follow-up work.

After informing and recruiting people to take part in the work, the project started with an introductory meeting, which was held to tell members about the project and about outcomes.

People spoke about what their disabilities were and what support they needed. They watched the Shaping Our Lives video and talked about the idea of direct payments. The members of the group were interested in finding out more. One person in the group had had direct payments but found them too complicated.

Another issue was the question of what it meant to be disabled. Some people were not able to identify what being disabled really was and what determined them being classed as a disabled person.

The group was also asked to think about two things that they would like to achieve. The answers ranged from being able to get up in the morning, to getting the right care, to going out to work.

This meeting set the scene for the project. It was attended by 12 people.

Two further meetings, which focused on care services and transport issues, were held. These were both attended by 12 people.

The bulk of the work focused on visits to members in their homes.

The issues addressed by the project

Care services

Most people thought that the care they received could be improved. At the introductory session one person said:

> I don't think that I'm receiving the right kind of care but I don't know what to do about it.

Other members supported this. They wanted to be able to live in their homes so that they had the freedom to do what they wanted, when they wanted.

They asked for home care services that were culturally aware and understood the needs of ethnic disabled people. One member had this sort of service and said that he was very pleased with the support given.

Other meetings identified some specific issues.

- *Home care*: several members were concerned about cleaning services for their homes and they were put in touch with EDGE's own home care service that has been set up by EDGE.

- *Social services*: members had a number of problems with social services. These were mainly about staff coming late, staff cancelling appointments and issues around language barriers. The development worker contacted the social services department but it did not respond during the time of the project. When the worker followed up the contact she was told that the department had lost the details.

- *Direct payments*: following the use of the Shaping Our Lives video in the introductory session, there were some discussions of direct payments. There was some interest along with concern about the possible complexities of employing personal assistants.

The development worker investigated the issue but further work is needed.

Help with odd jobs at home

Members talked about problems with odd jobs at home – changing light bulbs, minor repairs and the like.

As a result, the development worker met with the local Care and Repair service, the branch of a national charity that helps with exactly this type of problem. Information was collected and given out to members.

Transport

Discussions of transport brought out some positive and negative outcomes.

Members praised the city's Ring and Ride Service. The nature of the service – picking people up from their own homes – was highly valued. Participants also praised the staff who run the service for the assistance they give to passengers.

After this discussion, the development worker met with the Ring and Ride Service and helped people who were not already members of the service to join it. Later in the project, some members were experiencing problems with the Ring and Ride minibuses arriving late to pick people up and the development worker met again with staff at the service to address the problem.

Conversely, Manchester's new tram system was seen as being of very limited use. While it is physically accessible, people felt unable to use it as they do not live close enough to the routes.

One user voiced concerns about the voucher scheme in Manchester that gives people with mobility impairments subsidised taxi fares. The user complained that taxis often do not turn up when he calls for or books a trip. This issue has been taken up with the taxi company but they had not responded at the time of writing.

Heritage

Many of the members spoke about their history and experiences of coming to live in Britain and this led the development worker to contact the People's History Museum. There was discussion about putting on an exhibition at EDGE but this has yet to be arranged.

Contact was also made with the local adult education institute to find out about potential opportunities.

Other issues dealt with during one-to-one sessions

- Housing: extensive support to a member in dealings with housing officers.

- Difficulties with health services.

- Lack of information: meetings with members showed that many did not know where to get information and advice apart from EDGE itself.

- Accessibility: where people were aware of other services they did not feel that they were accessible to them. When speaking about their cultural problems and other issues, they felt happier dealing with an organisation run by people from the same background.

- Companionship: members valued EDGE's drop-in sessions as somewhere that they could go for friendship and to be around people from their own background.

Reports of two home visits

Visit one

The member told of how she came to England from Jamaica in December 1966. The thing that stuck in her mind was how cold it was and she felt like she was standing in a freezer. She had come to look after the two children of a friend who had died but she did not do this for very long. She had her first child, Lyn, in 1968 and her second, Winston, in 1970.

One of the many stories she shared was about going to a shop. She didn't realise that you had to open the door in order to go in. She stood outside the shop thinking it was closed as she was used to all the doors in Jamaica being left open all the time. She waited ages until someone went into the shop.

The member went on to tell a story of the experience of many West Indians in the 1950s and 1960s. It still brought tears to her eyes. She recounted moving to a flat in Didsbury and how she went to introduce herself and her children to the couple who lived upstairs, but they just shut the door in their faces.

She worked in Withington Hospital for many years and then left to look after her children.

In the early 1990s, she began to suffer from oesteoarthritis and high blood pressure. It became increasingly difficult for her to walk.

The only help that she seemed to get was from her doctor and he had referred her to social services. They sent out a social worker to see her but they told her they could not send anyone to do her shopping or laundry. She asked them about cleaning her home and was told that this was not essential. She was told that, if she wanted a home help, she would have to pay, which she did not mind. All they gave her was a list of telephone numbers and they left her to call people. That was the last she heard from social services.

The development worker informed her about EDGE's home care service.

Asked about how often she got out, she said that she went to three centres. She had to pay £4 to go to one of them, although it did not do anything for her apart from getting her out of the house. The centres were her only means of getting out of the house. She would not see anyone otherwise and felt lonely in the flat by herself.

She had not told any of the centres about the help that she needed.

The outcomes that she would most like to achieve are being rid of the pain that she experiences; to be able to get a home help as this would help her to maintain her independence. She believes that it should be her right to live in the home that she chooses.

At that time, she felt that no one seemed to be supporting her to be independent. Information was not readily available to her and she did not know who to speak to or where to go to find out about help.

She thought that the Ring and Ride Service should look at its policies regarding its services. At present, it offers its services only by pre-booking but it is not always possible to book if something happens and you need to use the service straight away.

Visit two

This member was 24 years old when she came to England by boat in the winter of 1954. She went straight to Bishop Street in Moss Side. She remembers it being very damp and her brother-in-law was living in the house where she got a room. Her first job was at Raffles clothing and she remembers that the pay was not very good.

She was joined later by her husband and her 14-year-old son, Vincent. Her mother, who was disabled, also came. She looked after her mother until she hurt her back. She went into hospital for an operation to repair the damage to her back but it was unsuccessful. This meant that she became disabled at the age of 42.

She registered as disabled after going to see her doctor when it became increasingly difficult to walk. She did not get any help from social services and in those days she did not know that she could get help from them. With no support available she just had to get on with life.

She did go to social security to ask for help but did not get any because she owned a shop. Although she had great difficulty making ends meet, she continued working until she retired. She received only £9 from social security.

She felt, if there was help, no one knew where to go for it.

After she retired, she had a nurse who came to visit her. The nurse thought her accommodation was unsuitable and found her a flat in a sheltered housing complex where she lived for a while. She was not happy there and decided to find somewhere else and now lives in purpose-built accommodation for elderly and disabled people.

She would like there to be more centres for disabled people. She goes to EDGE, which she enjoys as it is the only time that she is able to get out, meet people and find out what's going on. She would like to go out to more centres like EDGE and to have someone to take her there. She thought that EDGE would be better if there was more room.

She has a social worker and a home help who does cleaning and laundry. They do the work that she needs but the home help does not stay for the full hour. She also has someone who checks on her every morning because she has diabetes.

She feels very restricted about getting out and where she can go. She wishes there were people to help her to get out and more places where she could go. She had to give up going to one day centre because they were not able to guarantee transport for her.

Conclusion

The project was very popular with EDGE's members. There was such a high level of interest that we could have had meetings every week.

The project met key objectives of:

- bringing members of the ethnic disabled community together

- making other organisations aware of the needs of ethnic disabled people and the outcomes that they want to achieve

- developing the self-awareness of the group members

- starting to raise awareness of direct payments.

Members of the groups are beginning to feel that their lives are not such a struggle but there is a long way to go. There are also many more ethnic disabled people who could be part of this work.

A key issue for the continuation of the project will be ensuring that the work becomes as efficient and effective as possible. EDGE particularly wants to ensure that ethnic disabled people receive information and advice on the support that is available. The work of the project will also make a contribution towards recording the knowledge and experience of ethnic disabled people.

EDGE's work with Shaping Our Lives has achieved a great deal in this first year, but there is certainly much more to do.

References

Barnes, Colin, Mercer, Geoff and Morgan, Hannah (2000) *Creating Independent Futures: An Evaluation of Services Led by Disabled People.* Leeds: The Disability Press

Schalock, Robert L. (1995) *Outcome-based Evaluation.* New York: Plenum Press